Blue Rose

Patricia Jackson

Gotham Books

30 N Gould St.
Ste. 20820, Sheridan, WY 82801
https://gothambooksinc.com/

Phone: 1 (307) 464-7800

Published by Gotham Books (June 20, 2023)

ISBN: 979-8-88775-333-1 (P)
ISBN: 979-8-88775-334-8 (E)

Because of the dynamic nature of the Internet, any web addresses or links contained in this book may have changed since publication and may no longer be valid.

The views expressed in this work are solely those of the author and do not necessarily reflect the views of the publisher, and the publisher hereby disclaims any responsibility for them.

Contents

Look Inside

When the hurt is so much that you can't see through, there's a hidden light to turn on down inside of you,
through the midst of the abyss, when you look deep down inside, its what your made of that helps you glide,
so if you're going through some hurt or some doubt, remember its the end result that brings you out, out to a place you couldn't see before, a place you wont be afraid of anymore,
the strength that you find will be amazing, you see, as you look back and say, yea that was me,
a sudden pride of what you been through will arise, as you tell your story to help someone else through to the other side......

by: Patricia Walton

The pot of Gold at the end of the rainbow

The pot of gold at the end of the rainbow may be closer than you think,
it may be the hug of a precious love one or maybe in a cold drink,
it may be in the memory of a beautiful day as we capture a special moment & savor it in every way,
the pot of gold at the end of the rainbow may be closer than you think,
that new born baby, those special moments can go by in a wink,
capture the moment when you can, hold on with all you might,
don't take for granted those special moments, whatever you do, don't lose sight,
another moment will come while we wait for the next,
as we search for the pot of gold at the end of the rainbow,
this may be close as we get.

By: Patricia Walton

God is Poetry

God is poetry at its very best, even when we fail he passes every test,
God is big and he's small, he loves us one and all,
He's the Father, Son & Holy Spirit, how else can 3 equal one,
He's poetry in motion, just look & see,
from the highest mountain to the deepest sea,
God is poetry, He's the Alpha & Omega the beginning and the end,
what else can explain this majesty? This wonder in all his ecstasy,
Just look at the song of Solomon as he write about love,
His words came from God above,
God can touch the sick and make us feel fine, he makes us feel rich when we don't have a dime.
God is poetry at its best, we can lean on him to do the rest.
The rainbow is a sign of his poetry, as it reaches from one end of the sky to the other
its as if he is smiling down, as its bright colors touch the ground,
he says my children don't forget, I haven't forgotten you it not over yet,
Just like this rainbow you will see, soon all eyes will look on me,
I am poetry in motion at its best, I will return soon to show you the REST.

by: Patricia Walton

Ode to the tree

The tree is magic in its own way
as I stand tall wide, my branches wave as you go by, and I sway
from side to side,
my roots are deep and grounded strong & firm you see, I can't
be moved without the force of a great energy, and still my roots
stay put as I grow another me,
I stand in the rain 7 smile as it falls on my leaves, I soak up the
sun that shines so bright, it gives me energy,
You can use me as you please, make things out of me, pencils,
paper, furniture, wood houses, I'll do what you ask of me.
Birds use me to nest their young, I hold them nice & snug
between my gifted palms, Eagles soar above with wings spread
open wide, The owl sits & stares with such wisdom & pride.
As old as time I am and lots of stories to tell, you'll have to stand
the test of time and be strong as me as well,
people picnic under me & children play games around me, I'm
so glad to be a tree, I've always been and I will always be.
God made me, 'I'm glad he did and Adam named me Tree, I was
there when they hung my Lord, they used a part of me,
I tried to be strong as he was nailed on, but it hurt a part of me,
they hung him high and stretched him wide that was the day
even a tree cried (the weeping willow)
but I stayed right by his side, oh yea unknown in history, I the
tree have always been and I will always be.

by: Patricia Walton

If I were an eagle

If I were an eagle, I would soar the open space, I would spread my wings & glide, not a worry would I carry, I soar with such pride, and I'm not in a hurry,

God even wrote about me and gave you a view of what it's like to be free, to soar like me he said "you shall mount up with wings of eagles,"

being strong as I glide along with joy & ecstasy, I see things clearly from a different view, high above the problems that seem to overwhelm you,

if you rise up high like me, you can look down and see, You'll looks at those problems from a different view, through the eyes of Jesus they'll seem small to you.

You'll be able to soar and see what its like to be free of worry & hurt that's beneath you, you deserve the best of everyday, so look at things from a different way.

Rise up and look down and you will see, the battle is not yours because you been set free, than you will rise and soar and glide, and you'll run to the problem instead of hide.

By: Patricia Walton

Young Man

*Young man with your pants hanging low, I know you been
labeled so & so, but I know your loved by someone, because
when I see you I see my son,
when I see you passing by, I say a prayer & send it high, Father
protect that young son from the dangers of the streets, give him
knowledge & wisdom and help him pull up his pants for me,
I know your loved by someone when I see you walking by,
because when I see I see my son and it brings a tear to my eye,
I see the young man walking down the street, pants hung so low
almost to his feet,
I can't understand the reasoning of this new fad, I wish they
wouldn't do it because it looks real bad,
his shirt's to big, his pants to long, wait a minute is that my son?
I say another young man that same day, funny how he was
dressed the same way,
maybe that's my son, from a distance I could not tell, but he's
somebody's son, his parents love him just as well,
when I see that young man walking down the street, I'm afraid to
go over & speak,
young man, while you run this race, it's sometimes hard to keep
up the pace, it's hard to see beyond your stern face,
the love you keep hidden down inside, because you got to play
the role to survive,
young man on the go-I know you been labeled so & so, as I see
you going by, I say a prayer and send it high, God's Holy
protection as you go through,
keep you safe from the trap that's been set for you, be wise
young man in all you do & know that somebody is praying for
you..........
dedicated to my sons & grandsons*

by: Patricia

A fight on your hands

why do we fight & kill each other? that's not what we should do,
it doesn't take long to find out life has a built in fight for you,
don't hurt the ones that's struggling to do the same as you,
fight catching the bus at 5 a.m to get to where you got to go, fight
school & college, fight staying focused "you Know"
Fight staying focused on your goal& not get side tracked, when
you win this fight you'll know that someone had your back.
why do we fight & kill each other when we are in the same boat
together, fighting against the storm & weather,
fight not arguing & hurting even when you know your right, fight
not being promoted when you tried with all your might,
fight temptation not to sin when the world throws it in your face,
surrender to the will of God in order to win this race,
don't worry life has a fight for you, you'll see when the bills are
bigger than the check and everything is due,
fight doing right, when you're uptight and tempted to do wrong
Let the Lord fight your battle and you won't go wrong.

by: Patricia

Strength

I get my strength from God above, he sends it each day anew,
I need this strength to face each day because I might run into
you,
when the need to encourage others come my way, I depend on
the strength of God to tell me what to say,
I cant get my strength from you, because you are human too, but
when we join hand in hand and agree as one, on his word we
stand,
you can depend on me and I on you, because our strength is in
the truth.

by: Patricia Walton

Jupiter

Every time I turn around

Every time I turn around God does something new, The angles bow down at the very thought of you,
Blessed going in & Blessed going out, that's what I'm talking about,
Holy protection all around, when my enemy rise up they just fall down,
my foundation is solid as a rock & Jesus is my cornerstone, he is where I run to my shelter from the storm
Every time I turn around, God does something new, from every breath I take & every move I make,
the health & strength I enjoy so much, the hug I get from a gentle touch,
the bills seem to get paid somehow, the past is a vapor the future not yet come, all we have is the here and now,
every time I turn around, God does something new, Even the Angles bow down at the very thought of you.

by: Patricia Walton

What Say U

What say u, how shall I ask? You want me to accomplish this
task, where is my faith?? You ask,
my faith is shadowed & covered with fear: My faith is far instead
of near,
it's not as strong as it should be, can you get this blindness off
me?
Faith comes by hearing you Hold Word, I'll drown myself in it
till I'm purged.
I won't move from this spot until you show, Satan think he got
me where he want,
but you Lord, say "it isn't so…I'll wallow in your word like a pig
in mud,
I'll rise up clean "washed in the blood" and the moral is fo I let
u go, I don't got time for this blindness no mo.
Jesus come fo I lose my mind, fill this void while there's still
time,
Got work to do, got souls to save,
My Master have already paved the way.

By, Patricia Walton

Mountains

How many mountains do I climb in a day, the mountains of
obstacles along the way,
the mountain of traffic as I find my way through as I try my best
to get to you.
the mountain of problems I seek to solve, as I pray to God
because my brain can't hold it all,
the mountain of people, some smile some frown, the mountain of
holding on to hopes & dreams- I pause, that's a tall mountain
but its for a cause,
The mountain of expectations of a brighter day, as I try to hold
on to what I already have as I climb all these mountains from
day to day,
don't step on others along the way I don't have to go far to the
mountains I climb,
I just rise out of bed and be on my way.

by: Patricia

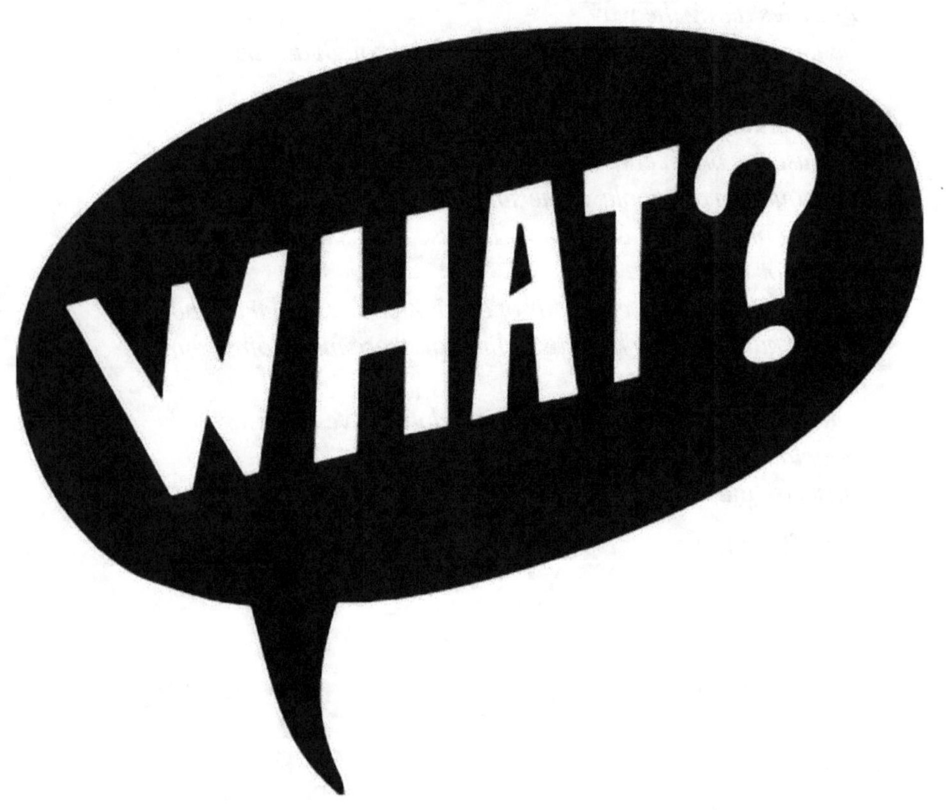
WHAT?

What does all this mean?

*God your love is astounding, I mean its totally the best, but
what's with all this other mess, is it some kind of test,
the good is good that's totally true, what pure, peace and
harmony I can find, I know it comes from you,
but what is all this other stuff? What does all this mean?
when I buy grocery, there's no person present I communicate
with a machine, the water faucet tell me when to wash my hands,
there's sadness everywhere, fear, terror, killings, earthquakes is
this all part of the plan?
I cant understand, what do all this mean?
you're all mighty and all powerful and I love you with all my
soul, you hold the world in your mighty hand, but nobody seems
to know.
Pants are sagging, people are nagging, everybody confused
about what to do, murder on a rampage, faith in you has been
severely damaged,
what does all this mean?
When the Bibles went out guns came in, look like saten got the
upper hand,-what a mirage, looks are deceiving, but show look
sad, people are hurting pretty bad and grieving,
sickness is on every hand, jails are full throughout the land,
people soul are being lost, perversion everywhere, crime is at a
all time high, people are dying without a care, we got barcode
here and barcode there soon a barcode everywhere, what does
all this mean?
teens are running in every direction, being diverted trying to find
a connection, everybody looking for something to hold on to,
would somebody tell them all we got is you? you're the only one
can carry us through this hype, and save us from this mighty*

*fright, in the midst of confusion everywhere, please tell them you
are still there, because this mess is a real nightmare,
abusing children for the fun of it, children suffering because their
innocent.*
Dear God- what does all this mean?

*People worshiping the wrong thing, celebrities praised for
nothing at all, Gods people overlooked liked they nothing at all,
one earns millions, while others suffer, its overwhelming, in the
midst of calamity everywhere, can somebody tell them that you
are still there?
where do we run to, to get away from this?, run to the rock, Lord
in the midst of chaos everywhere, would some body tell them you
are still there,
Read your word, and learn of you, say a prayer of protection as
we go through, Lord give us something to hold on to,
In the midst of confusion everywhere, can somebody tell them
that you are still there.*

by: Patricia

The Color Blue

*Mesmerizing so hypnotizing, capture the moment in the color
blue, peace and harmony creeps in and settles on you,
capture blue in a diamond, just stare & watch it shine, wrap
yourself in royal blue then feel the security and beauty combined,
the awe, the radiance, the royalty & appearance, reach for the
meaning, the statement it makes, confidence & assurance,
This color is surely a sign of endurance, look at it in awe,
wonder what it holds, when we see the color blue it looks so
bold,
take this color and wear it, ride in it, and feel the blue, as it
settles on you,
Blue must be the color of wisdom because it holds so much, try it
on- but you better hold on, and just feel the touch,
this must be more than just a color because it holds so much.*

by: Patricia

The purple side of heaven

*This side of heaven is reserved for people who helped others
along the way, through this life of trail they gave a helping hand,
they gave a cold glass of water to the thirsty, they fed the hungry,
they gave good advice when they couldn't help, their heart weep,
where the meek shall be satisfied, the humble shall be exalted,
the purple side of Heaven reserved for those who were left out of
the click, criticized, laughed at & looked down on because they
didn't fit,*
*where the meek shall be satisfied, the humble shall be exalted,
where those who hunger & thirst after righteousness shall be
fulfilled, where the merciful shall be shown mercy.*
*after the 144 thousand there is a number that no man can
number, these are those who didn't fit, when it came to being in
the click, their name didn't get called although they gave their
all in all,*
*their heart acked for what was right but no one noticed them
when they cried through the night,*
these are special in Gods eyes, he will comfort in due time.

by: Patricia

www.ingramcontent.com/pod-product-compliance
Lightning Source LLC
Chambersburg PA
CBHW050622160726
48003CB00003B/1299